Four Holiday Favorites

arranged for harp by Sylvia

Frosty The Snow Man

Let it Snow! Let it Snow! Let it Snow!

Rudolph The Red-Nosed Reindeer

Silver Bells

FOR LEVER HARP PLAYERS:

If you play a lever harp, be sure to set your sharping levers for the key signature before you begin. Also follow the additional instructions at the beginning of the advanced version of *Silver Bells*. All other sharping lever changes are written <u>between</u> the treble and bass staves. (The markings for pedal changes for pedal harps are written <u>below</u> the bass staff. If these confuse you, you can white them out.) This chart shows the octaves indicated for all of the lever changes you'll find in this book.

FOR PEDAL HARP PLAYERS:

You can use these songs as the basis for your own more complex arrangements. You're welcome to add additional notes to the chords, or add arpeggios and glissandos wherever you feel they will be appropriate. Pedal changes are written below the bass clef staff. The changes written between the treble and bass staves are for lever harps. If these confuse you, you can white them out, or highlight your pedal changes so they're easier to see.

FINGERINGS

Fingering preferences are very personal. The fingerings I have provided will give you a guideline from which to start. Feel free to change any of them if you'd like. It won't hurt my feelings at all!

THE "FEEL" OF THE PIECES

Most of these pieces have an indication of ♫ played as ♩♪ at the beginning. This just means that whenever there are two eighth notes, the first one should be held just a little bit longer than the second. This is the way these songs are usually sung, so you'll probably find yourself doing it naturally. For example, in *Rudolph the Red-Nosed Reindeer*, the beginning of the phrase "used to laugh and call him names" is not sung in a straight time of "1-and-2-and" etc. The words "used" and "laugh" are held longer than "to" and "and". Just play the pieces the way you *feel* them, and you'll probably be right!

With many thanks to Paul Baker, Don Snyder, Shirley Nute, and Patti Strout

Copyright © 2000 by Sylvia Woods, Woods Music & Books, Inc.
PO Box 816, Montrose, California 91021 USA
www.harpcenter.com

ISBN 0-936661-31-3

Frosty The Snow Man
easy arrangement

Harp arrangement by Sylvia Woods

Words and Music by Steve Nelson and Jack Rollins

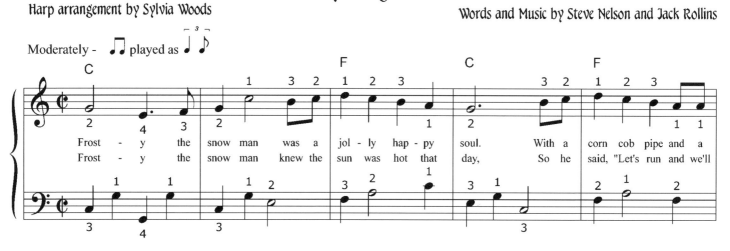

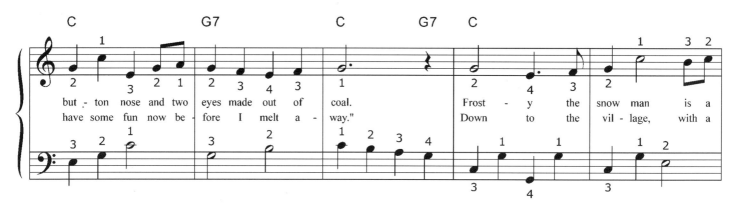

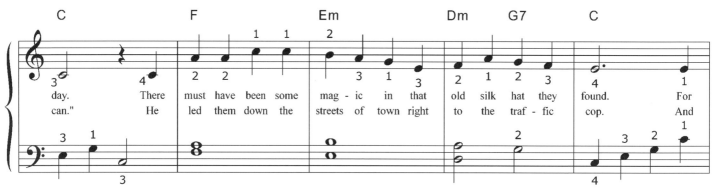

4

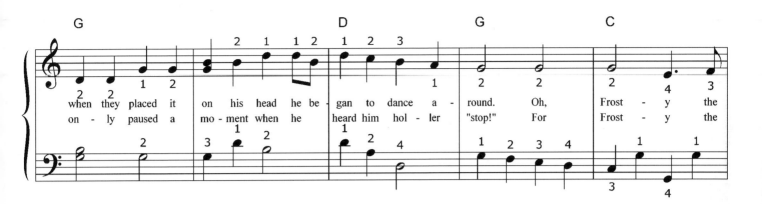

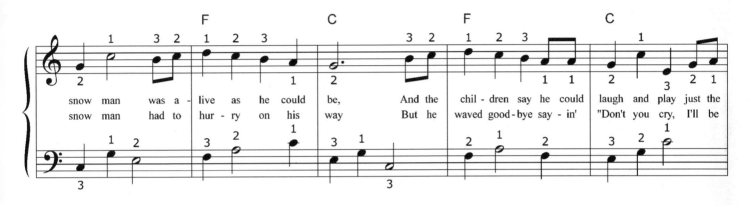

Frosty The Snow Man
advanced arrangement

Harp arrangement by Sylvia Woods

Words and Music by Steve Nelson and Jack Rollins

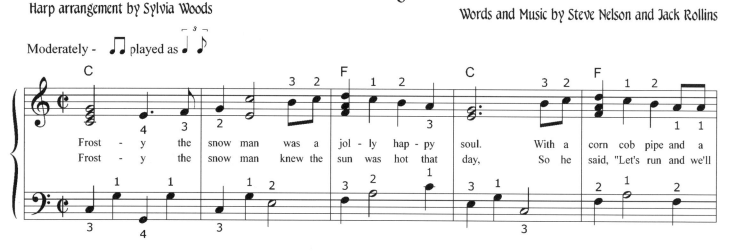

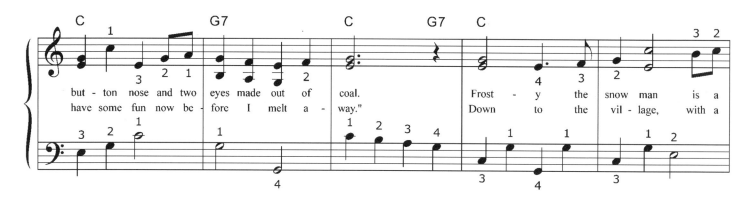

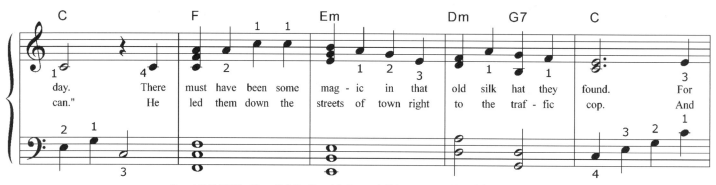

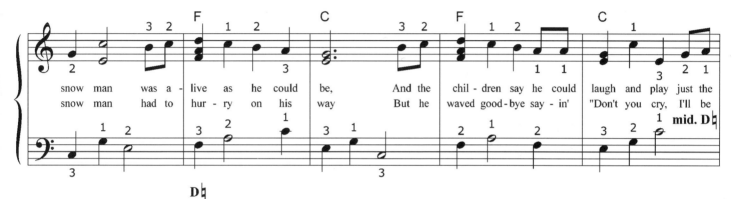

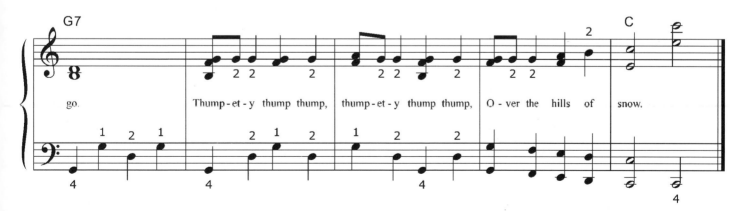

7

Let It Snow! Let It Snow! Let It Snow!
easy arrangement

Harp arrangement by Sylvia Woods

Words by Sammy Cahn
Music by Jule Styne

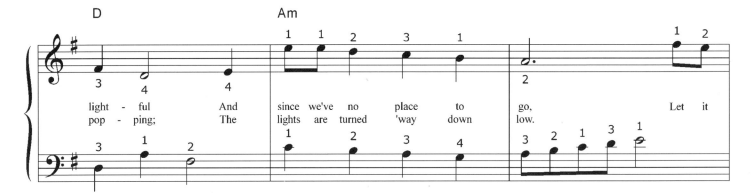

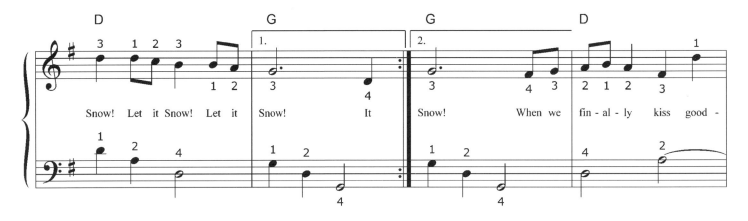

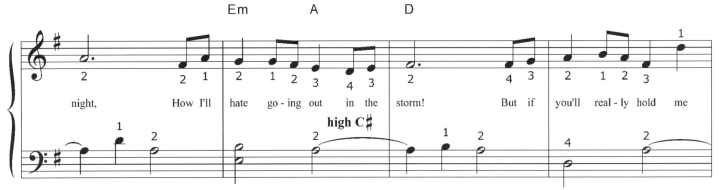

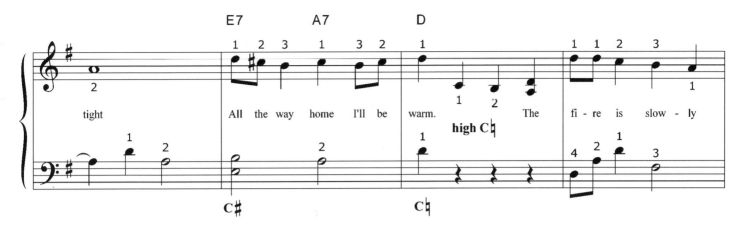

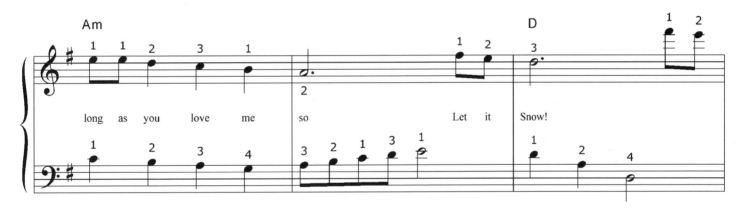

9

Let It Snow! Let It Snow! Let It Snow!
advanced arrangement

Harp arrangement by Sylvia Woods

Words by Sammy Cahn
Music by Jule Styne

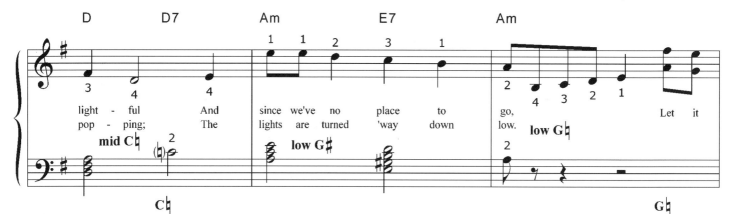

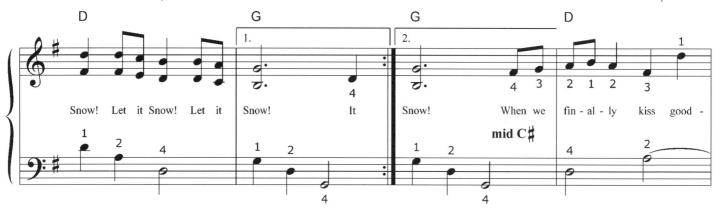

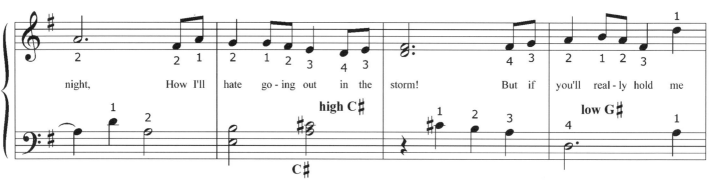

10

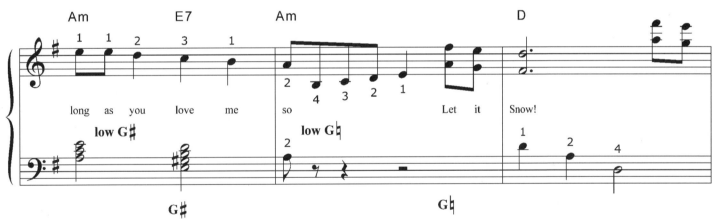

Rudolph the Red-Nosed Reindeer
easy arrangement

Harp arrangement by Sylvia Woods

Music and Lyrics by Johnny Marks

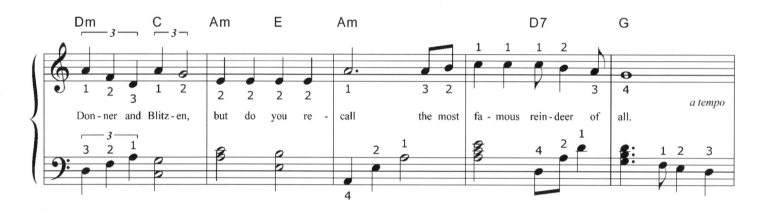

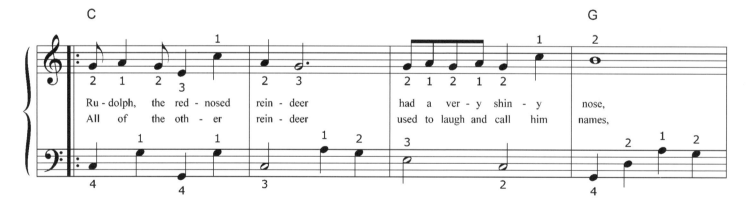

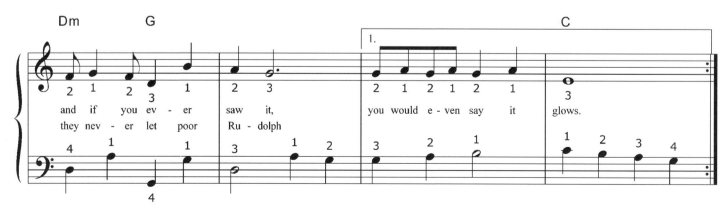

Rudolph the Red-Nosed Reindeer
advanced arrangement

Harp arrangement by Sylvia Woods

Music and Lyrics by Johnny Marks

Lightly -

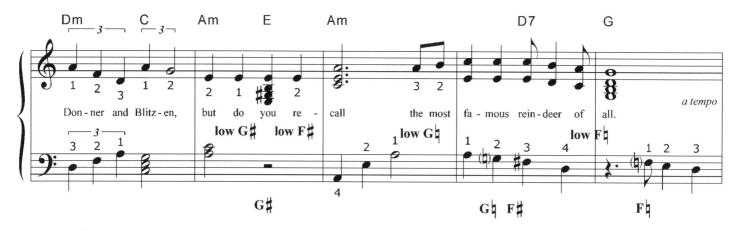

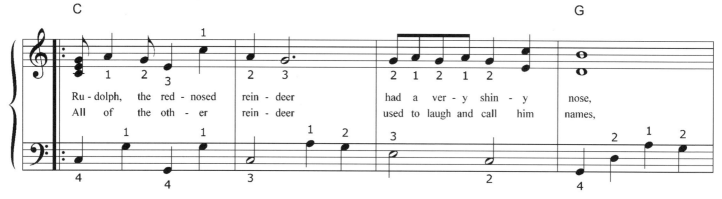

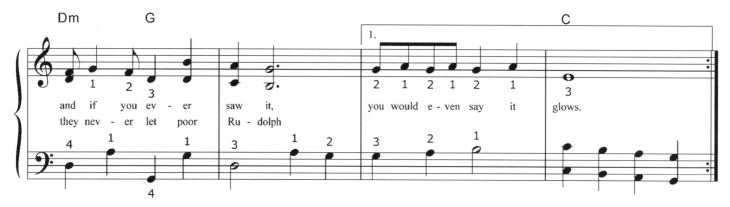

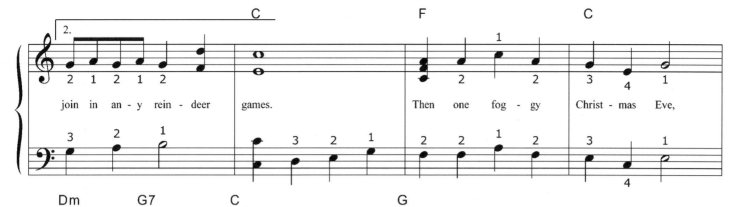

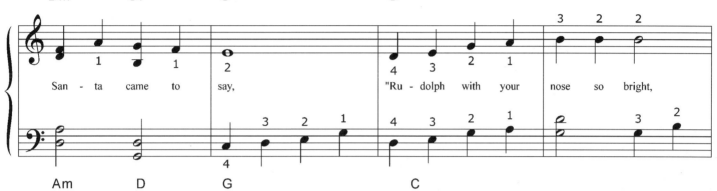

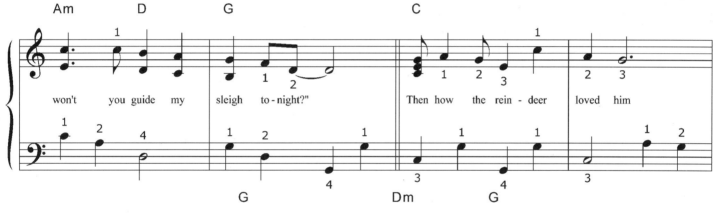

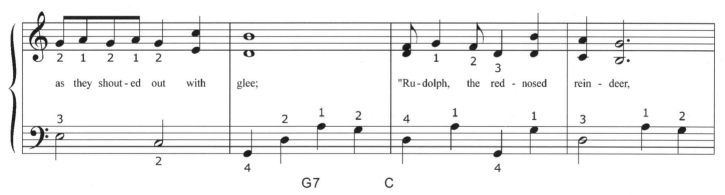

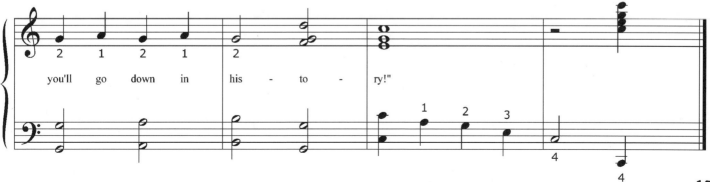

Silver Bells
easy arrangement

Harp arrangement by Sylvia Woods

Words and Music by Jay Livingston and Ray Evans

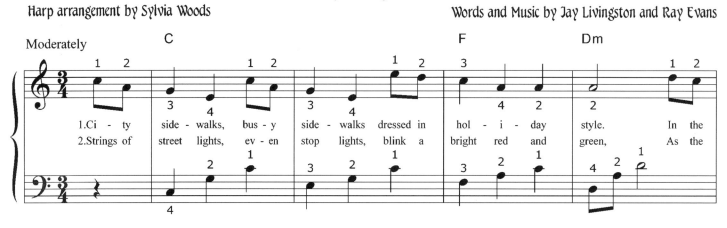

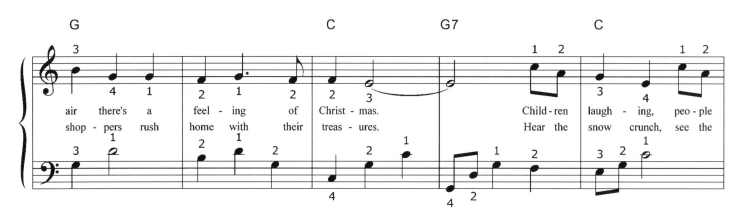

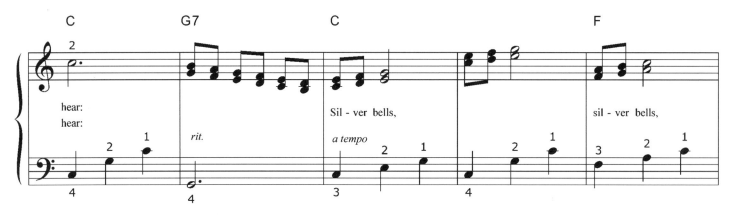

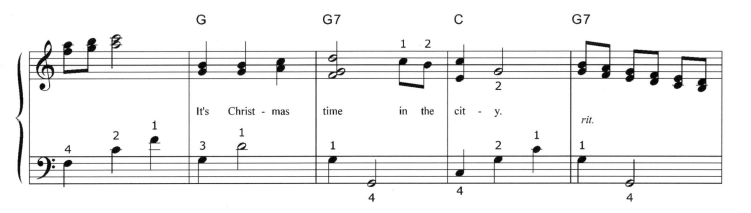

It's Christ - mas time in the cit - y. *rit.*

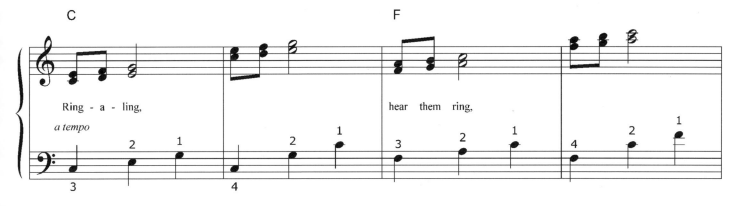

Ring - a - ling, *a tempo*　　hear them ring,

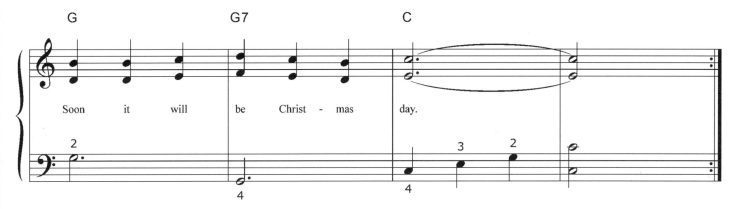

Soon it will be Christ - mas day.

Silver Bells
advanced arrangement

Harp arrangement by Sylvia Woods

Words and Music by Jay Livingston and Ray Evans

Lever harp players who have their harps tuned to C will need to tune the B right below middle C to a B-flat before they begin.
If you do not want to do this, you can play a middle C rather than the B-flat.

The rest of the lever changes in this piece are very quick F-sharps to F-naturals.
Engage the lever for the F-sharp, and then keep your hand on the sharping lever. Disengage the lever right before you play the F natural.

Lever harp players set the B-flat right below middle C.

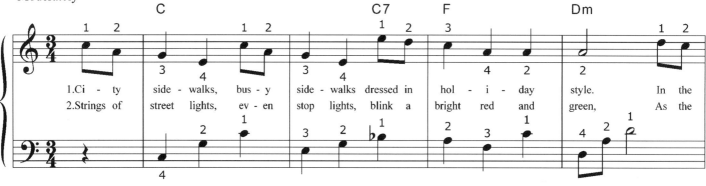

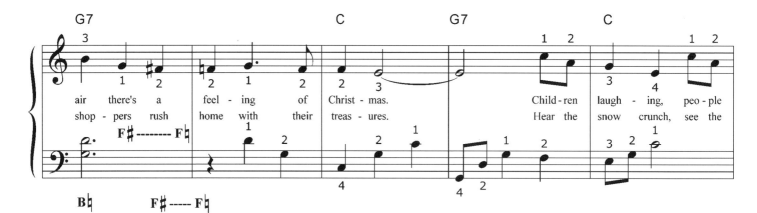

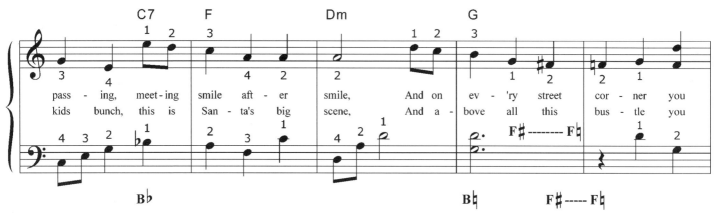

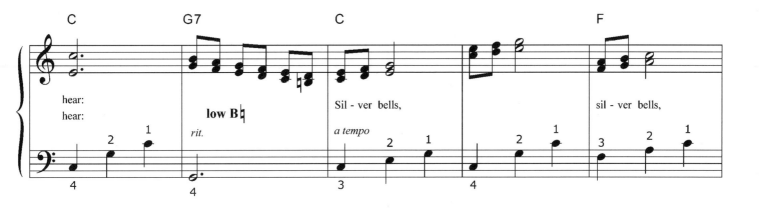

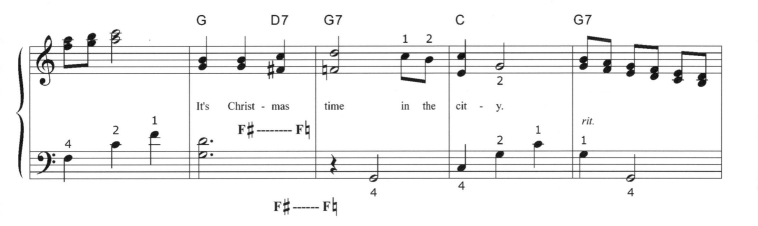

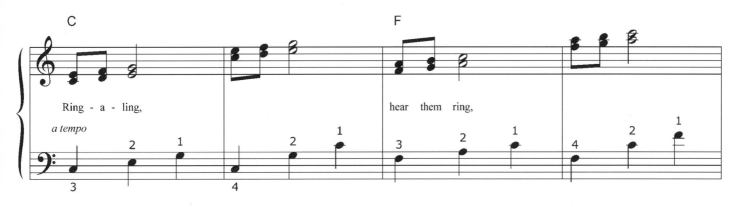

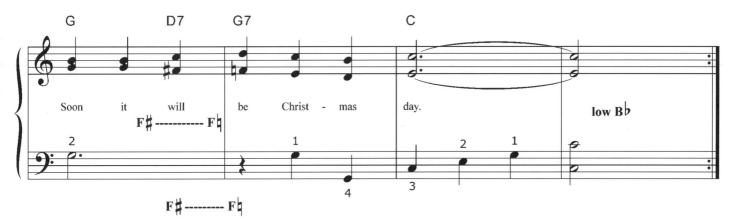

Other Books by Sylvia Woods

Music Theory And Arranging Techniques For Folk Harps
Hymns And Wedding Music For All Harps
John Denver Love Songs For The Harp
Teach Yourself To Play The Folk Harp
Lennon and McCartney for the Harp
Andrew Lloyd Webber for the Harp
50 Christmas Carols For All Harps
40 O'Carolan Tunes For All Harps
Irish Dance Tunes For All Harps
52 Scottish Songs For All Harps
50 Irish Melodies For The Harp
Chanukah Music For All Harps
76 Disney Songs For The Harp
Jesu, Joy Of Man's Desiring
The Harp Of Brandiswhiere
Beauty And The Beast
Pachelbel's Canon
Songs of the Harp

Sheet Music by Sylvia Woods

Simple Gifts
Winter Bells
Wondrous Love
Dead Poets Society
The Water Is Wide
Two Christmas Medleys
All The Pretty Little Horses
Love theme from Titanic: My Heart Will Go On
House At Pooh Corner / Return To Pooh Corner
America Medley: America and America The Beautiful
Spiritual Medley: Motherless Child and Wayfaring Stranger